Get Grounded!

35 Simple Ways to Balance Your Body, Mind and Spirit

by Harmony Rose West

Other books in Soul-Full Self-Care Series:

Calm Down!

Celebrate Now!

Nurture Yourself!

Available at HarmonyRoseWellness.com and Amazon.com

Disclaimer

Copyright 2014

This book is written to help adults and children ground so they can live healthier and happier lives. Although much is shared from the traditions of shamanism, energy medicine, hypnotherapy, meditation, and visualization, the author is not a medical doctor.

None of the information contained herein is to be construed as medical advice. Please consult your doctor as necessary before making any lifestyle changes.

With that disclosed, it is intended that the information contained in this book inspire you to live your life with more calmness, consciousness, presence, grace and ease.

Harmony Rose West

Table of Contents

Introduction

In the western world, we are accustomed to wearing shoes, walking on pavement, driving in our cars, and flying in airplanes. Too often, we completely eliminate the possibility of making a deep connection with our earth for days, weeks, even years. Consequently, we become disconnected – disconnected with our rhythm, with our surroundings, with our earth.

To bring ourselves back to a place of wholeness and secureness, we need to *ground*. Simply said, that means to be connected to the earth. We are all physical beings who would perish without our connection to the planet we inhabit. We need to let our metaphorical reach go deep down into the soil, we need to allow the soles of our feet to kiss the earth, and we need to cultivate our relationship with the earth that so lovingly supports us.

In Clint Ober's book, *Earthing*, he shares that many of the illnesses of modern man have to do with our loss of contact with the earth. He, along with many others, believe that a healthy dose of earth contact – earthing – is a powerful form of healing, and that with a healthy dose, many of these ailments can be avoided and even cured.

Our addiction to over-thinking, as well as our earth-deficient, hectic lifestyles, contribute to the stresses we experience. I've included many ideas that will assist you in bringing your energy down so that it's not overly congested in your head. Like the trees, make a decision to strongly anchor your energy to the earth.

There are actually three ways to think of Grounding:

1. **Physically Grounded**

   This includes being connected to the electro-magnetic field of the earth. It's how you live and move in your own unique physical vehicle while, simultaneously, feeling a connection to the planet you live on.

2. **Emotionally grounded**:

   How are you connected to your emotions? Do they move through your body freely or do you stifle your sad, mad or afraid feelings? The more you release, the better you feel and the more joy you can hold.

3. **Spiritually grounded**:

You are so much more than a physical body. Your body, mind, heart and spirit work best when woven in harmony and aligned with each other. Don't you feel stronger when you know you are connected to a power greater than yourself? Don't you like your day better when your heart is open and you feel blessed to be alive?

Any and all of the exercises in this Soul-Full Self-Care guide are good for you and can be done anytime. Especially consider grounding when you are --

Anxious or stressed

Spacey or light-headed

Disconnected or can't relate to others

Feeling stuck

Having trouble listening, learning or focusing

Having trouble walking or balancing

Not feeling emotionally supported

Picking up energy from others

Not feeling connected to the earth or a higher power

It is strengthening to physically, emotionally, and spiritually ground yourself. Let's begin!

~It is no use walking anywhere to preach unless our walking is our preaching.

St. Francis of Assisi~

What is Soul-Full Self-Care?

Soul-Full Self-Care is about giving yourself small acts of kindness right now!   It's about **intentionally** focusing on tender acts of self-love.

Soul-Full Self-Care is not meant to be a one-shot fix. Self-care is most effective when applied in small but constant doses; a few minutes here and a few minutes there. They are sustainable, cumulative practices that calm the stress in your body while nurturing your spirit.

Soul-Full Self-Care is taking care of your own energy, being responsible for your unconscious habits and changing them so you feel supported in this beautiful life.

Soul-Full Self-Care uses the healing energy of your hands and your thoughts to strengthen you.

Soul-Full Self-Care rituals bring you back to the present moment, this precious now, where all of your power is. It's about being here, instead of there.

Soul-Full Self-Care is taking time to tend to your body, mind, heart, and spirit so you can walk strongly on your sacred life journey.-

Soul-Full Self-Care is treating your Divine body as a priority. It's travelling deliberately down the roads of your life while also caring for the vehicle that's getting you around.

Soul-Full Self-Care is choosing to nurture yourself in little ways on a day-to-day basis, rather than tending to massive wounds down the road.

So, if you feel like you are galloping through your life, and you know you could use some **Soul-Full Self-Care**, you're in the right place.

One act of **Soul-Full Self-Care** leads to another. Just take it one day at a time.

Breath

1. Deep Conscious Breaths

Who doesn't need soothing? We live in such a fast-paced, over-stimulating world. How many times a day do you find yourself out of your body, out of your mind, out of the present moment? How connected to the earth are you when you are in this state?

Everyone can benefit by developing healthy methods of self-soothing to use when under stress.

Your breath is the most useful tool you own. It's free and readily available, though usually taken for granted. Deep breaths carry life-giving oxygen to your brain so you can think more clearly, relieve stress, and vent feelings. Just taking deep breaths helps to ground and center you.

Consciously choose to use this source of immense power and strength. It only takes a few moments to breathe intentionally and feel centered and grounded again.

SOUL FULL self care

Today when you feel anxious or agitated, take a few slow, deep breaths. Consciously focus your awareness on the air going in your nose and out your mouth.

See if you can get your breath all the way down into your belly. Hold it a moment before exhaling.

You may want to give a little audible sigh on the exhale to release tension.

Experiment with taking conscious, deep breaths anytime during the day, whenever you need some soothing influence. Feel how much more calm and grounded you feel.

~Of all the things that exist, we breathe and wake and turn it into song. Author Unknown~

2. Fear and Love

Challenges are a part of living on this earth. Maintaining a high vibration regardless of what comes at you during the day is a true spiritual practice. Embrace the notion that every challenge is an opportunity to learn something about yourself, and your world and your power to help others (and yourself) increases.

Why not have faith that your life is unfolding just as it should? It feels relieving to have faith that every situation has a purpose. Truly, no one can make you suffer. You are the only source of your happiness and well-being. While others can contribute, you must be the one that finds harmony on your Earth walk.

Find a quiet place to take a few moments to yourself. Close your eyes and as you tune into your breathing, feel gratitude for this life on this planet at this time.

Gently scan your body for any fear, tension or tightness. With each exhale, breathe out fear, negativity, limiting beliefs, stress, and pain. Decide that it is easy to let them go.

With each inhalation, feel the energy of love filling in the spaces where fear and stress lived. Allow yourself to surrender to the idea that love is easy and natural. Relax and ground as this peaceful feeling of love fills your body, mind, and heart.

See if you can hold this love as your walk into the rest of your day.

~How people treat you is their karma; how you react is yours.
    Wayne Dyer~

3. Expelling the Venom

It is hard to feel connected to the earth when you are so filled with energy that your head feels like it could explode.

Sometimes you feel too full from yummy stuff like staying up late to look at old photos, having long heart-to-heart talks, or celebrating getting an overdue but well deserved raise.

Sometimes you're doing yucky stuff like worrying about money, having a fight with your mate, or not knowing where your kid is and it's past curfew.

Here is an energy exercise that supports the release of emotional and mental overload. Once you've let go of so much, you will feel more connected to yourself.

SOUL FULL self care

Stand with your feet about shoulders' width apart. Tune into your level of overload. Feel it. Then, lift both your hands in front of you with your palms up. Visualize your overload and stress accumulating in your hands. Inhale and swing both of your arms up over your head.

Exhale as you forcefully swing your arms (palms down) down *expelling the venom* of your stress into the earth. Take another deep breath and repeat. Do it a third time, this time doing the motions very slowly.

Take a short...or longer...walk outside, or take a few moments to stand outside, and feel how much better you feel.

~Envy the tree, how it reaches but never holds. Author Unknown~

4. Focused Breath Meditation

You can do this breath before you pick up your children up from school, while sitting in the doctor's office, or even at a red light.

Sit comfortably with your spine straight and arms and legs uncrossed.

Feel your feet on the floor.

Eyes can be opened or closed.

Inhale to a count of four. Hold your breath for two counts. Exhale to a count of four.

With each inhalation, feel the healing influence of this focused breath.

Breathe this way for a few moments, and notice how much calmer you feel.

One or two minutes of focused breathing can make a world of difference in your day.

~Seeking life everywhere, I found it in the burn of my lungs.

Author Unknown~

Earth Contact

5. Bare Those Feet

I just moved to a beautiful piece of land 30 minutes north of Santa Fe, La Cueva Creek. It was a dry little arroyo creek bed when we arrived, but it's been raining for about five days now. The rain has turned this dry creek bed into a raging river, so full that it took out part of the dirt road that goes to my house. So, I've been kind of stranded, if you will, but in a good way. It has helped me to really appreciate the energy of the land and has given me time to stop and feel the earth under my feet.

In Traditional Chinese Medicine, at the bottom of the foot there's a point at the beginning of the kidney meridian called the *wellspring of life* or *gushing spring*. It's this point which really helps to establish our connection to the earth, to feel safe and less fearful. Energy from the earth is carried up the kidney meridian, to other meridians, supporting our health and well-being.

As I stand barefoot outside on our land, the moisture is palpable, and the air is clean and crisp. As I take a deep breath and bring my awareness to my feet, I can feel an exchange of energy happening between me and our planet.

I feel grateful for the connection I have (we all have) to the earth.

I believe if we could see this energy, and some can, we would see our *gushing spring* well up to overflowing. We would see that just like we have a relationship with trees (what we exhale, they thrive on and vice versa), we have a very real relationship with the earth.

This exchange is what we refer to when we speak about earthing or grounding. When we get wrapped up in our heads – thinking, thinking, thinking, we need to be outside. We are all healthier with a good dose of earth-touch.

SOUL FULL self care

Find a piece of earth, somewhere, anywhere near where you live. Remove your shoes and socks and stand on that earth. Bring your attention to the bottom of your feet, to your *gushing spring*. Imagine you are a tree and that roots grow from your feet, anchoring you to the earth. Feel how strongly rooted you are to the earth as you stand there.

As you go on about your day, remember, no matter what happens your roots are there to help you stay grounded. Like a tree, you will be flexible and able to withstand the storms that come your way, because you are aware of the relationship you have with the planet.

Stay in tune with this relationship by walking barefoot as much as you possibly can.

~The journey of a thousand miles begins with a single step.

Lao Tzu~

6. Hug a Tree

Trees... They are wise, living organisms with which we have a symbiotic relationship. We breathe oxygen, their waste product, and they thrive on our carbon dioxide. It's a worldwide exchange. Not only that, but an enormous amount of our food is grown on trees: apples, pears, cherries, pecans, walnuts, avocadoes – the list is quite long. They are dear to us. They are dear to me.

Many years ago, I was sitting in the dentist's chair, scared out of my mind, because he was going to pull a tooth. Sensing my anxiety, the good doctor asked what I needed to feel better so that he could do his job. Without even skipping a beat, I blurted out, "Hug a tree!" "Well, I think that sounds calming ... and doable," he replied. He guided me to a small outside area, complete with a few trees. Not caring what anyone else thought, I wrapped my arms around a tree and had myself a good cry. The tree felt like such a strong ally. Long story short, my fears were absorbed by the tree, the novacaine kicked in, and my tooth came out easily. Remembering the teaching of an American Indian friend to always leave something for the Earth if you take something from her, I buried my tooth under the tree as my token of thanks.

SOUL FULL selfcare

Find a tree someplace where you can have a bit of privacy. You don't want to waste your precious time and energy worrying what others think of you. If you truly aren't worried about it, freely pick a tree wherever you please. Wrap your arms around the tree, and take time to feel the life within this enormous plant. Feel the exchange of life taking place between you. If you need, ask this ally to absorb some of your fear, worry, pain, and frustration. As you hold the tree, feel your release running down the tree. Feel it travel down the roots and into the earth where it will be absorbed, recycled, and grown into something beautiful. Afterwards, leave a token of appreciation to the spirit of the tree – a piece of hair, a fingernail anything.

~Beneath most headaches is a heartache. Author Unknown~

7. Rosemary to the Rescue

All over the world for millennia, many cultures have taken advantage of the power of rosemary. In ancient Greece, students would place rosemary sprigs in their hair while studying for exams because it was thought to increase one's ability to learn. In old England, rosemary was believed to fortify the memory.

Today, rosemary is proving to help improve moods, boost immunity, increase circulation, ease inflammation, and much more. From steeping it in water for use as a hair rinse to rubbing the herb's oil on the body to alleviate pain, this herb is finding more practical uses each day.

Rosemary contains "rosmarinic acid," which has been known to be useful for healing asthma and breathing difficulties as well as for curing weaknesses of the brain. By increasing blood circulation to the head and brain, it improves mood and relaxation and is beneficial for lowering anxiety and depression.

Elena Avila, an Incan medicine woman, once told me, "If rosemary is growing in a garden, you can be sure a healer lives in that house!"

So whether you buy rosemary at your local grocery store or you grow it in your own garden, this healing plant is a great self-care ally to have.

SOUL FULL self care

Bring something to mind that is troubling you, something you would like some relief for, some stress you need to put down so that you can get on with your day. Now, gently rub your hands over a rosemary plant or rub rosemary into the palms of your hands. Inhale as you bring your hands to your face, and exhale, letting the tension drain out of you. Rub the rosemary again and as you inhale, bring your hands up to the top of your head. Exhale as you pull your hands down your body releasing your tension. Do this a few more times. Be mindful as you purposely let go of your stressful thoughts and feelings.

~We must release the old to make way for the new. Alan Cohen~

8. EarthBound

Research indicates that electrons from the earth have antioxidant effects that are able to protect your body from inflammation and its many well-documented health consequences. Most of us have lost contact with the Earth since substances like asphalt, wood, rugs, and plastics separate us from this needed contact.

It is known that the earth maintains a negative electrical charge on its surface. When you are in direct contact with the ground by walking, sitting, or lying on the earth's surface, the earth's electrons are conducted towards your body, bringing it to the same electrical potential as the earth. Living in direct contact with the earth grounds your body, inducing favorable physiological and electrophysiological changes that promote optimum health.

Your immune system functions optimally when your body has an adequate supply of electrons, which are easily and naturally obtained by bare skin contact with the Earth.

Multiple studies document that connecting to the Earth improves many stress-related conditions.

SOUL FULL self care

Find a quiet place and sit or lie down on the earth.

Tune into your breathing and notice the rising and falling of your chest as your breath enters and exits.

Give yourself as many minutes as you can to absorb this life-sustaining energy.

Carry this earthy energy with you into the rest of your day.

~Wisdom tells me I am nothing. Love tells me I am everything. And between the two my life flows. Nisargadatta Maharaj~

9. Belt Flow

There is a powerful energy that flows around the waistline, known as the belt flow. This free-flowing energy can become stagnant and hardened due to our sedentary Western lifestyles and lack of grounding to the earth. Instead of being a free-flowing energy, the belt flow becomes a boundary, much like a wall, between the second and third chakras. This barrier inadvertently cuts off the energy connection between the two energy centers.

Your will or ego is the dominant energy of the third chakra while spontaneity, trust and faith live in the second chakra. A stagnant belt flow hinders communication between the two.

Many people struggle with self-doubt and low worthiness Establishing a strong belt flow, connects the two chakras so self-condemnation begins to dissolve, and a deeper connection to a truer, kinder, gentler self can begin to grow. This simple exercise deserves to be in your self-care toolbox.

SOUL FULL self care

Pull across your waist from left to right, then cross the
midline and pull your hands down both sides of right leg.
Repeat in opposite direction and pull energy down your
left leg.

Teach your partner how to do this exercise, and then do
it on each other. Experiment with doing a belt flow while
you are standing, lying down, on your front or back of
your body.

Every hour, walk away from the computer and take a Belt
Flow break!

All of man's problems stem from his inability to sit in a room
quietly by himself.
Alan Cohen~

10.   Four Thumps

Your body accepts the energy of tapping because the beating of your heart feels, in essence, like a sort of tapping.

When you tap certain places with your fingers, your energy is impacted in a positive way because strong impulses are sent to your brain.

These Four Thumps work in tandem to strengthen your energy systems, move your energies forward, and re-charge your battery.

Let's do the Four Thumps:

1. Cheekbone Thump: While you breathe deeply, with the pads of your fingers, gently tap on both cheekbones beneath both eyes for 10 to 15 seconds.

2. K-27 Thump: To locate these important points, place your fingers on the valley at the bottom of your throat where a man would tie his tie. Go down about an inch and out about an inch and tap in those soft spots under your collarbone for 10 to 15 seconds.

3. Thymus Thump: Tap with your fingers in the center of your sternum, right on the thymus gland for 10 - 15 seconds. Children love the thymus thump, banging their chest like a gorilla, complete with sound effects!

4. Spleen Thump: Beneath the breasts and down one rib are the spleen neuro-lymphatic points. Tap them firmly for 10 to 15 seconds.

AS YOU TAP, notice if any places are tender. Those sensitive places need some TLC and will benefit greatly from your tapping touch.

~If you lose your mind, you will come to your senses. Fritz Perls~

11.   Grounding on the Hurry Up!

It's nice to have a grounding technique memorized so that you can keep in your back pocket to use whenever you need it. This is easy to do and will help you feel connected and anchored in less than a minute.

Quick Physical Grounding Technique

Do a hook-up: Put the middle finger of one hand in your belly button, the other middle finger in between your eyebrows on your third eye. Push in and pull up gently while taking three deep breaths.

Place your hands at the sides of your waist.

With your thumbs in front, slide your hands slowly and firmly down your legs.

Squeeze the sides of both feet as you hang for two deep breaths.

How easy was that?!

~Self-discipline is when your conscience tells you to do something, and you don't talk back.
W. K. Hope~

12.   Spinal Suspension

When you are feeling stiff because you've been sitting too long at the computer, the Spinal Suspension can be just the thing you need to loosen up. This exercise stretches and elongates the spine as well as opens up the shoulder blades.

In just one or two minutes, you will feel more space in that body of yours and rejuvenated and ready to rock and roll again!

The Spinal Suspension looks and feels like you are sitting on an invisible chair...

Stand with your feet shoulder-width or more apart. Place your hands on your thighs above your bent knees and straighten your arms. Take several deep breaths.

Adjust your feet so your knees are directly above your ankles and your arms and back are straight, like a suspension bridge.

Slowly stretch one shoulder across and down toward the opposite knee. Switch shoulders and repeat. You will feel a stretch across your back with this cross-over exercise. Stretch at least two or three times.

Slowly return to a standing position with your arms hanging by your side.

Feel how much more open your body feels.

~There is only one thing that makes a dream impossible to achieve: the fear of failure. Paulo Coelho~

13.   Spoon Your Feet

Do you ever feel a little scattered and ungrounded? As silly as it sounds, spooning the bottom of your feet with a stainless steel spoon helps ground your energy to the earth. It helps establish a strong electro-magnetic connection between the metal in your blood and the planet you live on.

Spooning your feet is a wonderful thing to do when you feel light-headed or have been around lots of electronics or other strong energetic fields. Working in front of a computer screen all day or flying in a plane can really scatter your energies, and this simple strategy can help you land again.

Spoon your feet if:

    You feel ungrounded;

    Your feet are sore;

    You've been out of contact with the earth for a while;

    You are exposed to electronics;

    You change time zones

    You feel light-headed or not in your body.

SOUL FULL self care

Let's do it! Find a stainless steel spoon and rub the bottom of your bare feet with the back of it. Make figure eight patterns or circles.

Rubbing the spoon across the bottom of your foot for about 1 minute encourages solid grounding.

This is a great little exercise to add to your everyday routine, especially if you suffer from sore or aching feet.

~Your task is not to seek for love, but to seek and find all the barriers within yourself that you have built up against it.

Rumi~

14.　　Wayne Cooke Posture

The Wayne Cooke Posture is a useful tool when you are overwhelmed or hysterical. If you need to untangle inner chaos, see with a new perspective, focus your mind, think more clearly, or learn something new, this is an invaluable exercise to have in your self-care toolbox. If you need to teach or be on in front of a lot of people, this exercise will help you find peace and balance beforehand.

This exercise is named after Wayne Cooke, a researcher on the field of bioenergetics force fields.

Sit straight in a chair. Place your right foot over your left knee. Wrap your left hand around your right ankle and your right hand around the ball of your right foot. Breathe in slowly through your nose, letting the breath lift your body as you inhale. Gently, pull your right leg toward you, creating a stretch. Breathe and stretch three times.

Switch sides. Place your left foot over your right knee. Wrap your right hand around your left ankle and your left hand around the ball of your left foot. Gently pull your left leg toward you, creating a stretch. Breathe and stretch three times.

Uncross your legs and place your fingertips together forming a pyramid. Rest your thumbs on your third eye, the space in between your eyebrows. Breathe slowly in and out three times. Then, exhaling out your mouth, let your thumbs separate and slowly pull your fingers across your forehead, really opening up your forehead. Bring your hands to your chest in a prayerful position while breathing deeply. Feel how balanced you feel.

~There are two ways to feel wind: climb in to the open and be still or keep moving. Author Unknown~

15.   Connecting Heaven and Earth

Sometimes we just need to move!   You know when you've been on the computer too long, and your thighs feel like they are glued to the chair? The energy in your joints feels stuck, and you absolutely need to get up! You feel sluggish and your saner mind knows your cells could use a healthy dose of oxygen.

Stretching and reaching toward the sky while also reaching for the earth feels great. Connecting heaven with earth is a metaphor that could have far-reaching benefits in your life. This exercise activates endorphins and supports feelings of joy. It stimulates the immune system and will help you feel energized and refreshed.

Connecting Heaven and Earth is one of the most popular energy medicine exercises because it helps you feel better quickly. This powerful stretch opens the energy channels called meridians and quickly helps you feel renewed and refreshed.

SOUL FULL self care

Let's connect heaven and earth! Standing, rest your hands on your thighs.

Inhaling through your nose, bring your hands to a prayerful position at your chest. Exhale through your mouth. Inhale and stretch one arm up and one arm down, pushing down with your palms as you hold your breath. Hold, hold, hold. Now exhale as you return to the prayerful position.

Repeat, switching arms. Then bend over and relax with slightly bent knees. Take two deep breaths, return to standing position, and feel yourself connected to both heaven and earth.

~I stand straight in your presence. I hold my head up high.
With my feet rooted in Mother Earth.
My arms embracing Father Sky.
Walks Tall Woman from *The Thirteen Original Clan Mothers*
by Jamie Sams~

16.   Lather Up!

Those of us in the western world have the luxury of bathing or showering daily. Not only does the water cleanse away our dirt and grime, but the essential nature of the element of water has the potential to wash away our tensions and fears. Let those troubles go down the drain!

After you bathe and dry off, instead of just rubbing lotion on thoughtlessly, what if you added some gratitude to your lotion? Tuning into your body and honoring it with gratitude when nothing is wrong (you haven't just bumped your knee or cut your finger) is a powerful way to communicate with your body temple.

Here's how to add some really powerful medicine to your morning ritual of putting on lotion.

SOUL FULL self care

As you apply lotion to your skin, thank your body for its strength, vitality, and vigor.

Thank your arms for all the hugs you give, thank your belly for all the food you digest, thank your knees for all the steps you take, thank your face for all the emotions you express...you get the idea.

Appreciation is a wonderful *free* soothing skin balm.

Adding gratitude to your morning routine doesn't take any more time. It adds consciousness to this simple everyday action.

Affirming your strengths is cumulative and has the ability to transform your relationship with your body.

~We could never have guessed, we were already blessed, where we are. James Taylor~

17.   Fifteen Seconds

The earth is our mother. Each of us must take care of her.

We depend on this planet for our survival, and she, in turn, depends on us.
Without her, every single one of us would perish. She offers food, water, air, trees, bees, and so much abundance. All this bounty is often taken for granted.

All life forms on earth are to be treasured. Every inch of the earth is sacred. Often we forget that and unconsciously harm her. Wouldn't you like to give praise to Mother Earth rather than have her feel unappreciated?

Just as you flourish with appreciation, so does our living planet. Why not begin a new relationship with the planet you live on?

SOUL FULL self care

Take fifteen seconds, and re-connect to the Earth.

Say a prayer of thanks before you eat your meal.

Put your feet on the ground.

Be conscious of breathing in air you usually take for granted.

Open your refrigerator, and thank the earth for growing all that food,

Thank the water as you brush your teeth.

Feel grateful for the reconnection and bring it to the rest of your day.

~If you had a sad childhood, so what? You can dance with only one leg and see the snowflake falling with only one eye. Robert Bly~

18.   Begin Again

This is it! Whether it's the warmth of the sun that kisses you awake or the blaring of your alarm, it's here. Today is here. It's time to welcome the wonder of a brand new day. Instead of battling through the grogginess, instead of dreading the workload you have to get through today, instead of anticipating your awaiting struggles, enjoy the fact that you are given the chance to live another day. You are able to remain in your body and to experience this day and all its beauty. You are able to invite new experiences, to create new opportunities, to love, listen, and live. Today is a chance to begin again. Greet it with arms wide open. Embrace it with the deepest welcome.

SOUL FULL self care

First thing in the morning, walk outside and stand barefoot on the earth (or imagine you are outside). Take a deep breath. Do it again. Breathe in this new day, and exhale any worries or problems. Then, bend down, and touch the earth. Say a prayer, a word of thanks, admiration, and appreciation to her: *Dear Mother, thank you for all the bounty you provide to all of us. Food, water, air, trees...we are so dependent on you. I deeply thank you for all the ways you contribute to my life.*

Stand up and feel your feet planted firmly on the ground. Now reach up overhead with both arms open wide, declare your anticipation for this day as you stretch and reach towards the sky: *Source of all things, Creator, Father Sky you who are called a thousand names yet are truly nameless, I welcome the synchronicities and miracles of this day.*

Exhaling, lower your arms, and bring your hands to your heart, and feel the marriage of the earth and sky in your heart chakra. Connecting with Mother Earth and Father Sky at the beginning of your day is a sacred act of grounding in your day.

~Those who contemplate the beauty of the Earth find reserves of strength that will endure as long as life endures. Rachel Carson~

19.   Cloud Gazing

A group of girls and I gathered in the yurt for our weekly girls' circles. Munching on organic blue corn chips, we passed around our talking stick and shared what was on each girls mind. When it was seven-year-old Ria's turn, she called our attention to the ray of bright sunlight streaming into our space. Noticing that the sunlight highlighted the specks of dust in the air, we discussed the value of ear wax and boogers to protect us from all the unseen pollutants. Oh, the topics of children!

A while later, Ria laid on her back and called to us to join her and look out of the skylight. The clouds were gracefully dancing across the sky, and we enjoyed the shapes and movement. All the children and I were spontaneously enjoying the precious present moment together.

The very next day, my husband and I were in our loft, and he laid down on the futon. "Come join me," he encouraged. "Take a self-care break and watch these amazing clouds." We enjoyed about ten minutes of lying on our backs together, appreciating the beauty of the sky.

SOUL FULL self care

Lie on your back on the lawn, the porch, your bed looking out the window, wherever you can watch the parade of clouds passing in the sky. If lying down isn't possible, sit outside or where you can see out the window. Watch the grace and ease in the movement of the clouds. Notice how quickly the pattern changes. Notice how blue the sky is, the sunshine, or lack of it. Feel your breath breathing you as you gaze upon the clouds that we usually take for granted. Feel yourself connected to the earth as you take in the beauty of the sky. Spend a minute or two or three. Now bring this simple awareness of the beauty of the ordinary into your day.

~Staleness is sadness. Freshness brings joy. From the film Like Stars on Earth, produced and directed by Samir Khan~

20.   Getting Stoned

I absolutely love being barefoot. My feet aren't as white and sun-deprived as many, and they aren't as soft, but I wouldn't trade it. The feel of pine needles, sand, grass – wherever it is, my tootsies are happy to be skin-to-earth. Over time, they've become so sensitive that my feet yield with the presence of anything sharp underfoot. Conversely, they have also become hardier. I'm able to walk barefoot in places that amaze both my friends and me. The bottom line is that I enjoy feeling grounded. I love to know that I am connected to the earth. It's strengthening.

When I go into town, I can enjoy the pleasure of wearing my pretty shoes, but out here, it's bare, happy feet for me.

SOUL FULL self care

When I'm unable to enjoy my bare feet outside, I find my grounding indoors by placing my feet on one of the many grounding stones I have scattered around my home. If you aren't like me and don't spend a majority of your day barefoot, you can still ground and find strength throughout your day by doing the same.

Find a big flat rock that is large enough for at least one of your feet to rest on, and put it somewhere that you like to sit and spend time, maybe on the floor in front of the couch where you watch TV, or underneath your desk. I have stones scattered throughout my house in places where I can rest my feet and re-ground my energy.

Having one of these grounding stones near your computer or laptop is essential. I haven't done any measureable study myself, but experts (and my personal experience) say that putting your feet on a rock helps balance the electromagnetic energy from your computer and helps you feel grounded.

~Our life experiences will have resonances within our innermost being,
so that we will feel the rapture of being alive. Joseph Campbell~

21.   Put Those Worries Down

There once was a man who worked at a very stressful job. He knew that if he didn't find a way to de-stress, he would bring his worries home with him and possibly take his frustrations out on his family.

One day, he made a very deliberate decision. Before he walked into his house, he sauntered over to a tree. He took off his tie and hung it on the tree, letting it symbolically represent the troubles he was carrying, and that he was deciding to leave his troubles on the tree. The next morning, as he left for work, he took his tie off the tree, put it around his neck and once again, wore it to work.

SOUL FULL self care

Is your work day stressful? Do you find that you unintentionally take your work frustration out on your kids? Do you want to be able to be with your family as cleanly and with as much presence as possible?

Tonight, before you go inside your house, take a moment to leave your worries outside.

Touch a tree, touch the earth, dig a hole, put them under your car...whatever metaphor helps you to leave your troubles outside of your home. Your home is your sanctuary. It's where you should come to re-boot and re-fill your well. If you find you still need your work troubles, you can always pick them up tomorrow!

Sometimes I've believed as many as six impossible things before breakfast. Lewis Carroll~

Jon Kabat-Zinn, founder of the Mindfulness-Based Stress Reduction program at the University of Massachusetts Medical Center, defines *mindfulness* as paying attention in a particular way...on purpose, in the present moment, nonjudgmentally.

Purposefulness is a very important part of mindfulness. When you have the purpose of staying with your experience, whether it's being with your breath, or chewing, or walking, you are intentionally shaping the mind.

Left to itself, the mind wanders through all kinds of thoughts, mostly regurgitating negative thoughts over and over again. Most thinking is about the past or future. The past is done. The future hasn't happened yet, it's only a fantasy. The one and only moment we actually can experience is right here, right now. The present moment is the one we seem most to avoid.

So in mindfulness, we're concerned with noticing what's going on right now. That doesn't mean we can no longer think about the past or future, but when we do so we do so mindfully, so that we're aware that right now we're thinking about the past or future. Let's focus on being in the present as a deep act of grounding yourself.

Go outside for a walk. Take a few minutes or give yourself the gift of a longer walk. As you walk, mindfully focus on each step you are taking. Feel your right foot come down into contact with the earth as you say to yourself, I have arrived. As your left foot connects with the earth tell yourself, I am here. How simple, easy, mindful and powerfully grounding.

Bring this mindfulness into the rest of your day.

~There's more to life than increasing its speed. Gandhi~

Massage

23.   Massage Kidney-1

What an incredible structure the human foot is! Take a moment to consider how much weight your feet carry and all the activities you gallop through in the process of your daily routines.

Dancers and movement facilitators know how important the feet are to our health and well-being. Strong feet allow us to stay grounded as we walk...or dance... through our days!

The Kidney meridian or energy flow begins on the bottom of both feet. Kidney 1 or K-1 is the first acupuncture point, or "acupoint," on the kidney meridian. It's found right in the middle of each foot at the base of the ball of your feet. Having an open flow of energy here is essential to being able to be grounded to the earth.

SOUL FULL self care

After a shower in the morning, take one minute per foot to massage K-1. If you want, use a healing lotion or coconut oil. Put a little dab on the palm of your hand and let your body's heat warm it up to give extra pleasure to this foot massage.

Use your thumb and give a deep massage to these points. Then, flip your hand from one side to the other so the electromagnetic energy of your hand frees up any frozen energy.

As you rub your feet, declare things like, I am grateful for your support. You provide me a foundation for the gift of movement and the ability to move in grace. Thank you. Thank you. You could also add, I love you!
Make this a daily ritual. Your feet will love the attention.
Submitted by Deanna Watson

~How many cares one loses when one decides not to be something, but to be someone. Coco Chanel~

24.   Massage Those Tootsies

I am blessed that my husband loves to rub my feet. How great is that? As wonderful as that is, Bill isn't always up for the gig, so sometimes I have to take matters into my own hands, so to speak.

Once, we were hiking for hours. My feet felt like they were gonna just fall off. I knew I should have worn my other hiking shoes! What will it take for me to listen to my intuition? When we were back home, I pulled off my boots and made whimpering noises hoping Bill would tend to my aching feet. However, my partner had agreed to be our dinner chef and already had his head in the refrigerator. I sat on the floor and began to massage my aching feet. Moaning and groaning, I prodded around to feel what the damage was. The top of my feet felt like they had been squashed and restricted, so I tenderly began to rub. Soon, I was using more pressure, pushing my thumb into the top of my foot. Ah! I lingered longer in the sorer spots. For ten minutes, my aching feet were the focus of my life. I just knew that a little TLC right now would go a long way and soon, my feet would be back in the game of supporting me. By the time dinner was ready, I felt like I had a new pair of feet.

SOUL FULL self care

I'm sure you can stand to do the same. So, take off those socks and shoes, and sit for a few minutes – take a load off of those feet. However you can manage it, position one foot so that you can reach it. Grab your foot with your dominant hand so that your thumb is on top. Using your thumb, massage in a deep, circular motion the spaces in between the bones on the top of your feet. These spaces that run from your toes on up your feet are called gaits. As you massage, you open up the energy on the top of your foot, and it relaxes the soles so they can easily connect to the electro-magnetic field of the earth. Massage each gait (top of your foot) for a minute or so, and then switch feet. Your tootsies will love your forever.

~If you truly love yourself, you will love the person next to
you. Dr. Irvin Laszko~

25.   Stimulate Stomach 36

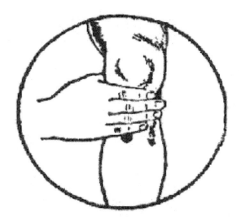

Stomach 36 or Leg Three Miles is the 36th acupoint on the Stomach meridian. It is said that if you are exhausted from a long journey, stimulate this point, and you will be able to walk another three miles.

In your day-to-day life, stimulating this point helps revitalize your entire system as well as supporting recovery from long term illness or stress.

Stimulating this point increases energy and builds strong blood. Stimulating ST 36 relieves all kinds of digestive ailments, abdominal cramping, bloating, and pain.

SOUL FULL self care

Let's work it! Stomach 36 is located just below the knee, on the outside (lateral) aspect of the lower leg. Place your hand just below the right patella (knee cap).

Feel for this point, on the outer surface of your leg, close to the tibia (shin bone), at the lower border of your hand.

Rub it hard as you breathe deeply. Massage this point throughout the day or when you feel that you need some revitalization.

~Being present means living without control and always having
your needs met.
Byron Katie~

26.   Thigh Massage

Our thighs take a lot of use and abuse. Sitting down, walking, standing, all involve the muscles of the thighs. As we stand on the earth, we take our totally-necessary thighs for granted.

Rubbing the large intestine neuro-lymphatic points, located on the outside of the thighs, helps get the digestive process rocking and rolling.

Whether you tend toward constipation or loose stools, neither of those two choices are balanced.

Focusing your attention, in addition with strong pressure along the large intestine neuro-lymphatic points helps balance your overworked digestive system.

SOUL FULL self care

Either stand, sit, or lie down...get comfortable. Using your fingers, massage up and down the outside of your thighs, pressing as hard as you are comfortable with.

Using deep pressure, massage from the knee to the hip and back down again.
If any spots are sensitive, it just means you need this massage.

Make sure you massage both thighs.

Sometimes, just standing with your hands on your thighs can help to connect you to the earth.

~Try not. Do or do not. Yoda~

27.   **Grounding Kegels**

When I was pregnant, my midwife stressed the values of doing Kegels. Kegels are pelvic muscle or pelvic floor exercises which consist of repeatedly contracting and relaxing the muscles that form part of the pelvic floor. This exercise is often prescribed for pregnant women to prepare the pelvic floor for the stresses of the later stages of pregnancy and childbirth.

Further research taught me that these exercises have also been shown to improve incontinence since they strengthen the muscles at your bladder outlet. They are also said to help improve sexual enjoyment.

Another more subtle benefit of doing Kegel exercises is that they strengthen the first chakra. Chakra means "wheel of light" and refers to the spinning vortex of energy created when magnetic energy from the molten core of our planet rises up and meets electrical energy descending from the cosmos.

These chakras or energy centers are said to propel our life force. The base or first chakra rests in the perineum at the base of the spine. This chakra is concerned with survival, stability, security, patience, and the ability to manifest your dreams. It is very worthwhile to spend a few minutes here and there strengthening this energy center.

SOUL FULL self care

Decide that you are going to do Kegels at red lights! What else are you gonna do while you wait? (If you don't drive, find another time you can do these)

Take a post-it note and write a "K" on it and put it on your dashboard. This will be your friendly reminder, an anchor that will remind you to do this new self-care habit.

Every time you are stopped at a red light, exercise those perineal muscles. As you inhale, pull up like you are trying to stop yourself from peeing. Then exhaling, release the muscles. Do these as many times as you have time for at the light. You are strengthening your pelvic floor and helping yourself anchor strongly in your root chakra.

If you want to live a strong and healthy life, it is imperative that this vortex of energy be grounded and vital.

~A young girl was drawing a picture of God.

Her teacher calmly told her that no one knew what God looked like.

Without missing a beat or looking up from her drawing, the child replied, "They will in a minute." ~

28. Everyone Poops!

Even if we blush talking about it, isn't it true that every single animal on the planet poops and pees out what it doesn't need? There's no escaping it. The children's book, *Everyone Poops* by Taro Gomi makes adults laugh, but children love this book. They are naturally curious about what's coming out the other end of them, and adults are hesitant to spend much time on this subject!

No matter how nourishing our food may be, our body cannot possibly use it all. If our digestive system is healthy, a potty release happens multiple times a day.

What if during our many visits to the porcelain throne, we took a minute to release some other things we no longer need? What if we released our negative thoughts towards ourselves, others, and our situations? What if we let go of all the worrying and obsessing that is regurgitating in our minds and intentionally focused on letting it go?

SOUL FULL self care

While you are sitting on the toilet, tell yourself, *I release anything that no longer serves me.* While you say this, imagine you are letting it all go.

Let go of your fears, your confusion, your anger, your stress, your hurt... EVERYTHING that doesn't benefit you.

Visualize it all being flushed down the drain with the rest of the waste.

Now, don't you feel a whole lot lighter?!

~If I had a prayer, it would be this: God spare me from the desire for love, approval, and appreciation. Amen. Byron Katie~

29.   Root Lock

The root lock, or Mula Bbandha, is a yogic practice. *Mula* indicates the base of the torso, the perineum. It is associated with the first chakra along the spine. The word *bandha* translates as to bond, connect, put together, unite, combine, or join.

In the root lock, muscles are tightly contracted at the center of the perineum. Contraction of these muscles is said to affect the nervous, circulatory, respiratory, and endocrine systems, and the system of internal energy, known as chi or prana. The root lock is calming, stabilizing, and enhances concentration.

Sit in an erect posture, preferably a cross-legged seated position. Close your eyes and relax your breath.

Contract all the muscles of your perineum and hold as long as you are comfortable.

Keep your breath as steady and smooth as possible, without pausing. While tension is being maintained, continue to breathe slowly and smoothly.

Now, changing gears, inhale as you contract the perineum, and exhale as you release the contraction. Time the contractions so that they coincide with your breath. Do this exercise 10-25 times.

As you get more experiences with this exercise, center your attention on the center of the perineum, and contract the muscles there tightly with minimal involvement of the anal area. Can you feel how the root lock is a simple, yet deep way to connect yourself to the earth?

~The same stream of life that runs through the world runs through my veins. Rabindranath Tagore~

30.   Bounce and Shake!

You probably give a lot more thought to maintaining your weight than to making sure your circulation is strong; but if you are interested in preventing disease and cleansing your body of toxins, pollutants, additives, and chemicals, your circulatory system needs to be robustly healthy.

Your heart is the power behind your cardiovascular circulatory system, pumping blood through your blood vessels, supplying every part of your body with the oxygen and nutrients it needs for proper functioning. With poor circulation, not only is your blood flow impaired, but your heart is overtaxed. These can lead to a variety of health problems.

It seems obvious that shaking and bouncing your body will get your blood pumping. Your lymphatic fluid is completely dependent on physical exercise, and the up-and-down rhythmic gravitational force caused by jumping on a trampoline causes the lymph system's one-way valves to open and close, increasing lymph flow.
Don't have a trampoline? What if you did some bouncing and shaking? This zero-impact exercise will increase your oxygen intake and help you detoxify through your lungs and skin.

SOUL FULL self care

Put some music on that has a great rhythm. Everything goes better with music! Stand with your feet shoulder-width apart and start to bounce and shake. Feel your feet flat on the floor, and notice how they keep you grounded as you move. Keep your knees soft, not locked. Let the music bring you more and more present.

Turn from side to side letting your arms flap. Work those shoulders. Move your hips from side to side. How does your head want to move? Experiment with what feels good. Your goal is to create enough movement that you can feel your heart rate and breathing increasing. Keep moving for the whole song. You can do it!

Don't you feel more energized? Your lymph system thanks you!

~Be patient toward all that is unsolved in your heart and try to love the questions themselves. Rainer Maria Rilke~

Visualization

31.   Grounding through the Chakras

Chakras are centers of energy, located on the midline of the body. There are seven of them, governing our psychological properties.

The first or root chakra is about being physically here and feeling at home in situations. If it is strong, you feel grounded, stable, and secure.

The second or sacral chakra is about feeling and sexuality. When it is open, your feelings flow freely, and are expressed without you being over-emotional.

The third or navel chakra is about your self esteem.

The fourth or heart chakra is about love, kindness, and affection. When it is open, you are compassionate and friendly.

The fifth or throat chakra is about self-expression and talking. When it is open, you have no problems expressing yourself.

The sixth or third eye chakra is about insight and visualization. When it is open, you have a good intuition.

The seventh or crown chakra is about wisdom and being one with the world. When this chakra is open, you are unprejudiced and quite aware of the world and yourself.

SOUL FULL self care

Sit with your feet flat on the floor. Keep your legs and hands uncrossed. Place your hands on your thighs, palm-up. Close your eyes, and taking a deep breath, bring your awareness inward.

Imagine, sense, and perceive a channel of energy funneling from your body into the earth. Let yourself drop into the feeling of support and connection as you open this grounding channel. Imagine a cord flowing from the bottom of your feet and reaching into the earth.

Feel grounded as you now imagine light brownish-red energy traveling up through the bottom of your feet.

Let this energy rise up from the feet into the calves, the thighs, your buttocks, and into your first chakra. Feel the deep connection as this color enters your first chakra.

Now, let this grounding energy rise into the second chakra, then into the third, the fourth, and up into your neck and head through the fifth, sixth and seventh at the top of your head. Sense this energy extending out into your arms and hands, flowing into your aura that surrounds your body.

Now, beginning with the seventh chakra imagine all of this energy moving downwards from one chakra to the next. Bring all of this energy back down through your whole body, dropping from the sixth, to the fifth, the fourth, into the third, the second, and into the first chakra.

Let it continue to flow downwards through your calves and your feet. Let all of the energy drain downwards, through your grounding cord and into the center of the earth. Open your eyes slowly and bring this grounding into the rest of your day.

~Your task is not to seek for love, but to seek and find all the barriers within yourself that you have built up against it.
Rumi~

32.   Grounding Through Your Heart

According to the HeartMath Institute, the heart produces the body's most powerful rhythmic electromagnetic field, which can be detected several feet away by sensitive instruments. The energy of your heart is exponentially wiser than your head's ability to figure things out.

Research shows your heart's field changes distinctly as you experience different emotions. Focusing on positive emotions can significantly alter your experience of stressful events.

SOUL FULL self care

When you are irritated by someone, someplace or something, stop and take a deep cleansing breath.

Inhale deeply through your nose, and put your hand on your heart. As you deeply exhale through your mouth, imagine, sense and perceive the irritated energy is being released down into the earth. Let this stress travel down through your belly, your hips and legs and feet, being drawn down into the earth. Do this a few times while you visualize the earth's magnetic field pulling your irritation into her core and easily transforming it into soil and trees.

Continue to breathe deeply as you keep your hand on your heart. Tune into the beating of your heart and feel how this strong electromagnetic pulsing energy radiates a loving, soothing, healing energy into your body. Walk with this lighter and brighter energy into the rest of your day.

~We come with all these parts and no instructions how they go together. Author Unknown~

33.   Leave the Past Behind

It has been said that guilt is not being in the present moment because of something that happened in the past, and that worry is not being in the present moment because of something that may or may not happen in the future.

Right now is the only gift of time you have. Maybe that's why it is called the present. So many of us spend useless time regurgitating past events over and over and over again. We regret something that we did or something that we didn't do. We feel bad about something that we said or something that we wished we had said.

Living with these past memories is harmful to you. Don't spend your precious life currency on something that has happened already. If you need to make amends to someone, be courageous and do what you need to do. It's simple, but not easy, yet courage is a value worth cultivating.

Decide to have closure with your past. It's over and done with. Give up hope for a better past. Teach yourself to be in the present moment, right here, right now. It's truly all you have.

SOUL FULL self care

Guided Imagery

Imagine, sense, and perceive in a way that is perfect for you. You are sitting in a motor boat that is zooming along in the ocean. Even though the waves are rising and falling, you feel strong and stable. The wind is blowing your hair, and you are appreciating the movement forward.

You look behind you and see the wake of the water that your boat leaves behind it as it travels forward. You realize that the past is just the wake of water that is behind you. Your past doesn't drive the boat, you do.

You are always supported in this vessel in which you are traveling. All you have to do is put your hands on the steering wheel. You smile as you remember all the times you feared the past was what was propelling you forward.

As the boat nears the shore, you understand and trust that you are moving towards a new vision and experience of yourself. The boat slows and finally docks. As you step onto the shore, you inhale deeply and breathe in trust for the next leg of your journey.

~Every experience is fertile ground for transformation and awakening.

Alan Cohen~

34.   Rooted to the Earth

A group of us were sitting in a circle, exploring what community means to us. We then participated in a drumming circle. Luisa Koelker, a local shaman and psychotherapist, led us through a powerful guided imagery. We imagined a grounding cord coming out the base of our spine reaching into Mother Earth like the roots of a tree. I had experienced and enjoyed this meditation before but Luisa expanded and continued to guide us. "Now imagine your roots are intertwining with other people's roots." She said. "Feel how connected we all are. We are not alone."

I thought of the huge redwood trees in California, considered to be the largest and tallest trees on earth. Some of these ancient giants are over 2,500 years old and rise three hundred feet high. One might think that these large trees would have a tremendous root system reaching down hundreds of feet into the planet. The redwoods actually have a very shallow system of roots, but the roots all intertwine, and so are locked to each other. When storms come or the winds blow, the redwoods support and protect each other.

SOUL FULL self care

Sit with your spine straight as you take a few deep breaths. Exhale tension and inhale peace. Now, imagine, sense, and perceive in whatever way comes to you a strong root coming down from your spine into the earth. Feel this root traveling down, down, down...even further down into the earth. Feel how strongly connected you are to the planet you live on. Just like a tree, you are rooted to the earth. Imagine your friends' roots are down there too. Consciously feel how easy it is for your roots to intertwine. We are all connected. We are family. When you are ready, open your eyes, and take this grounded and connected feeling into your day.

~Do not forget that the value and interest of life is to do ordinary things with the perception of their enormous value. Tellard de Chardin~

35.   Shower Yourself

When I was a girl, we lived at the end of a dead-end street with a forest behind us. One of my favorite pastimes was shimmying up the tall, thin trees, hanging and swinging like a monkey. For many years now, I've longed to be able to access nature like this, to have it right outside my back door.

As of a few weeks ago, this is my reality. We've moved to an amazing habitat of fluttering aspens, enormous ponderosas, and more oak than I've seen anywhere else in New Mexico. Twenty three acres of paradise and only a mere half hour away from town. My new home, complete with a lily pond, is my magical oasis.

The last few days have brought amazing rains, thunderous downpours such as these aren't very common in my neck of the woods. It's just rained and rained and rained. The rushing river created by these downpours has taken out part of the dirt road that leads to my house. My little Volvo hasn't the gumption to even try to figure another way out.

So, I'm here 'til the road is fixed. You could say I am stranded, but I prefer to think of it as a day out of time. Taking advantage of my leave from the hustle and bustle of the outside world, I went for a walk in the rain. I stood on the bridge with the fast-flowing water beneath me and imagined the current carrying away all of the stagnation out of me. I imagined my energy stream flowing as easily as this rushing river.

I felt my fear and worry being washed away by the pouring rain as it joined the raging waters below. I love my new home.

SOUL FULL self care

Either in the rain or in the shower, you too can experience this cleansing and freeing power. Just stand under the shower (or out in a rainstorm - preferably) and imagine the waterfall of cascading water has the ability to wash away toxins, worries, and stagnant energy.
As you visualize the bad stuff being washed away, feel your energy being freed up. Start to feel it flow more and more freely until it rushes free just like the water itself. Breathe in deeply a breath of gratitude for your release of these things.

~Sounds of the wind and sounds of the sea make me happy just to be me. June Polis~

SOUL FULL self care

Think kind thoughts about yourself often

Greet the sun...feel the wonder of a brand new day

Girlfriend, take your bra off while you're at home!

Take slow, deep breaths when you need soothing

Rub your own head, toes, feet, hands, arms

Walk barefoot as much as possible

Smile because you are alive

Doodle

Light a candle

Hug yourself often

Sit or lie on the earth

Laugh because it feels good

Breathe deeply into your belly

Have a picnic dinner on your bed

Pray for those with less than you

Bathe in gratitude at the end of the day

Go for a walk, even though your to-do list isn't finished

HarmonyRoseWellness.com

Review

If you feel that this book has added value to the quality of your life, I would love for you to take a few minutes to leave an honest review on Amazon. Your feedback helps others decide if this book will support them in living their best life.

All the best, Harmony Rose West

HarmonyRoseWellness.com

CPSIA information can be obtained
at www.ICGtesting.com
Printed in the USA
BVOW04s0237270917
496036BV00014B/158/P